Psalms of Exile and Return

BY KEITH HILL

CLASSICS OF WORLD MYSTICISM
The Bhagavad Gita: A New Poetic Version
I Cannot Live Without You:
Selected Poetry of Mirabai and Kabir
Interpretations of Desire:
Mystic Love Poems by the Sufi Master Ibn 'Arabi
Psalms of Exile and Return

POETRY
The Ecstasy of Cabeza de Vaca
The Lounging Lizard Poet of the Floating World

FICTION
Puck of the Starways
Blue Kisses

NON-FICTION
The New Mysticism
The God Revolution
Striving To Be Human

Psalms of Exile and Return

A journey in search of
inner healing and unity

Keith Hill

attar||books

Published in 2020 by Attar Books
Auckland, New Zealand

Paperback ISBN 978-0-9951204-5-7
Ebook ISBN 978-0-9951204-6-4

Copyright © Keith Hill 2020

Keith Hill's right to be identified as author of this work is asserted in accordance with Section 96 of the Copyright Act 1996.

All rights reserved. Except for fair dealing or brief passages quoted in a newspaper, magazine, radio, television or internet review, no part of this book may be reproduced in any form or by any means, or in any form of binding or cover other than that in which it is published, without permission in writing from the Publisher. This same condition is imposed on any subsequent purchaser.

Cover image: Jovan Vitanovski / Shutterstock

Attar Books is a New Zealand publisher which focuses on work that explores today's spiritual experiences, culture, concepts and practices. For more information visit our website:

www.attarbooks.com

CONTENTS

PREFACE   7

IN BABYLON

Invocation   15
The slave reviews his situation   17
In the temple of Baal   18
His captors demand the slave sing   19
The reality of life in Babylon   21
He is plagued by Baal's priests   22
The slave sighs for his lost beloved   23
He is awakened by a dream   24
The slave meets Daniel   25
Doubt still torments the slave   27
He perceives the nature of the world   28
The slave considers his heritage   29
He hears a voice calling him   30
Daniel teaches the way to escape   31
A dream causes wonder and confusion   32
The slave escapes from Babylon   33

IN THE WILDERNESS

The song of the good shepherd   37
The work of the good shepherd   39

The reality of life in the wilderness	41
Babylon's soldiers find the shepherd	43
Praise for Yahweh, goal and guide	45
The shepherd ponders the imponderable	46
He becomes the cry in the wilderness	47
He reaches the wadi of which he dreamed	48
The shepherd is reunited with his beloved	50
Yahweh, the shepherd's shepherd	51
The shepherd and his beloved resume	52
On the banks of the Jordan	53
Yahweh's gift of wisdom	55
The shepherd appreciates his beloved	57
Yahweh, the sole refuge	58
They see the walls of Jerusalem	60

IN JERUSALEM

They enter Jerusalem	63
The knowing servant's song	64
First song of the beloved	66
The servant weds his beloved	67
Second song of the beloved	68
The reality of life in Jerusalem	69
The unity of lover and beloved	70
Evocation	72

THE MYSTIC TASK OF REINTEGRATION   75

PREFACE

Exile involves physical displacement from one's homeland that, at the least, is profoundly disorientating, and at worst terrifying. Historically, exile has taken many forms. Politically, it was used to punish those who committed crimes or fell out with a state's rulers. Over the millennia many have chosen to go into voluntary exile to avoid being imprisoned or executed, while entire populations have been exiled from their homelands by war, famine and partitioning. Millions more have been conquered and transported to distant countries to live as slaves.

This last was the case when, in 587 BCE, Judah's King Zedekiah decided to join Egypt in revolt against Babylon. The army of Babylon's ruler, King Nebuchadnezzer, first defeated the Egyptians, then besieged Jerusalem. This was Judah's third rebellion against Babylonian rule in a little over a decade, so when the city fell no mercy was shown. King Zedekiah's sons were executed in front of him, he was blinded, and he and thousands of Judaeans were marched off to Babylon to become slaves. Jerusalem's city walls and its Temple were destroyed, and Judah became a vassal province of Babylon.

Exile slashed a permanent scar across the Judaeans' hearts. Their pain is recorded in many books, notably *Isaiah*, *Jeremiah*, *Daniel*, *Chronicles*, *Ezra*, *Psalms* and *Lamentations*. The overriding emotion was grief leavened with confusion, emotions encapsulated in a profound question: Why had Yahweh* allowed their kingdom to be defeated and their Temple destroyed? Judah's prophets answered that the Judaeans themselves were to blame, because they had wandered from their Lord's path. Yet no matter what was said, or where the responsibility lay, the Judaeans' exile continued. And as the years passed, their grief compounded. Worse, there was no apparent end in sight, leading the Judaeans to question the very purpose of their existence.

Last century, following World War II, a similar dissociation set in as the survivors processed the enormity of what human beings had done to one another: the Warsaw Ghetto, the siege of Stalingrad, the V2 bombings of London, the fire bombings of Dresden, the cruelties performed on captives, the Nazi death camps, the dropping of two atomic bombs—and these were just the most calamitous acts from six years of war in which over seventy million people died. Moreover, this occurred just two decades after World War I had killed twenty million and traumatised three generations. By the middle of the twentieth century many were wondering what had gone wrong with humanity. That a Deity believed to be all-seeing and all-loving had stood back and done nothing led many to question their religious beliefs. Or to jettison them completely.

The same state of disassociation was faced by the exiled Judaeans in Babylon. Their city had been sacked, their Temple destroyed, their world shattered. Facing a lifetime of slavery, they no longer had any certainty regarding the right way to live. Terrifyingly, many must have feared that the all-powerful Yahweh had instigated their exile, or, just as bad, approved of it.

Crises force people to find new meaning in their lives. In

---

* An explanation for the use of Yahweh as a name for God here follows shortly.

response to the catastrophic impacts generated by two world wars, twentieth century thinkers generated new explanations for human behaviour. One line of thought was provided by existentialism, a philosophy that responded to the moral and spiritual vacuum in which people found themselves. This included the realisation that people in positions of leadership, and those who followed them, were living inauthentically and making decisions in bad faith, resulting in humanity collectively becoming morally and spiritually exiled from itself.

Of course, there is a significant cultural gap between modern philosophers and the ancient Jewish prophets. Where twentieth century thinkers saw their situation as a crisis of existence, post-exilic Judaeans underwent a crisis of faith. The Temple around which their lives had long revolved was demolished. So what was their purpose now? Was Yahweh testing them? Or had He deserted them? And what were they to make of their new situation? They expressed their uneasy thoughts and feelings in vivid prophecies and pain-filled psalms, which in their honesty and heart-break continue to reverberate powerfully for us today.

The ancient poets' psalms express the full range of feelings that result from displacement and exile: rage, horror, gratitude, love, self-pity, celebration, despair, bitterness, awe. Their thoughts swoop from the tribal to the social to the metaphysical, while their words are alternatively introspective, tortured, dogmatic, confrontational and inspired. Above all, out of disturbed times and difficult lives, they conjured words of immense spiritual depth, beauty and power.

The psalms speak to us today because our world continues to be filled with great misery and suffering. Vietnam, Cambodia, Bosnia, Darfur, Rwanda, Congo, Syria, Sudan, Yemen—decimation and death have left populations traumatised. And in the world's cities, our so-called centres of civilisation, there is no escape: poverty, exploitation, violence and trauma abound. Our collective exile from our deep selves remains unchanged. We are no nearer to finding a way to reintegrate individually or collectively. We are no nearer to making a better world together.

The ancient prophets addressed this disruption, and its very necessary resolution, within a narrative that is simultaneously historic and spiritual. It is a narrative that begins in Babylon, physically a place of captivity, symbolically a site of psychospiritual disassociation, and it leads us to the new Jerusalem, which symbolises both an origin and a longed-for future state of integration, peace and grace. Psychospiritually, the new Jerusalem is the inward state in which our regeneration takes place. But the new Jerusalem only comes into existence as we work to reintegrate our psyche and unify what is currently dispersed. Using the words of the prophet Isaiah, we have yet to recognise our new heaven and new earth, let alone build on them, for they are the foundations from which will rise the inner new Jerusalem of the integrated human being.

These poems reflect that process of recognition and transformation. Drawing on imagery created by the writers of the *Psalms*, *Isaiah* and *The Song of Songs*, what follows is an attempt to outline an inner journey that is deeply challengingly, often extremely scary, yet ultimately takes us into the mystery of our selves. But it is a journey we need to make collectively, for one another. We are in this world together. Others will follow. It is for each of us, after we depart, to have let into this world at least a flicker of the light of Origin, the ultimate Source to which we all return.

I share with the ancient Jewish prophets the conviction that we are more than what we make of our selves; that our world is more complex, profound, and perplexing than what we, however sincerely, reduce it to; and that each of us has the possibility of journeying into this mystery and engaging it face-to-face. Thus, while the poems that follow draw on the ecstasies and laments of those ancient exiles, my hope is that they reflect a journey that is not just valid today, but that we can, and will, face up to, and set out on ourselves, individually and together.

ON THE NAME YAHWEH

Yahweh, written YHWH in Hebrew, is the name for God used here. The name YHWH dates to Mosaic times. Much later it was Latinised into Jehovah. By the third century BCE, practitioners of Judaism decided the name YHWH was too sacred for anyone but priests to use. Elohim (Gods) then became preferred for general use, along with Adonai (the Lord), translated in the Septuagint, the Greek version of the Hebrew Bible, as Kyrios, Lord. Other preferred names included El (God), Shaddai (Almighty) and Ehyeh (I Will Be). I chose the name Yahweh for these psalms as it is used in almost all canonical Hebrew texts. My hope is that it is at least vaguely familiar to English-language readers, while remaining untethered to specific theological positions.

Being untethered is important because all names are placeholders that point towards a greater reality. This can readily be seen in relation to human beings. An individual's personal name never encapsulates the full reality of who they are; it is merely a handy shorthand we use to reference them. However, the relationship between the name we use to identify and their reality can be complex. If we don't know a person, or only possess a cartoon sketch of them, then their name conjures limited meaning for us; but if we know them well, hearing their name conjures a rich blend of meaning. Adding to the complexity, our relationship with others is often developmental. As we get to know them better, learning about their history, gaining insights into what they think and feel, and so discover why they do what they do, the feelings and ideas their name conjures in us when we hear their name changes. The reality we associate with their name becomes more nuanced and layered. In practice, this means that when we hear their name, we project both what we know of them *and* what we subjectively feel and think about what we know onto them. Yet neither their name, nor our projected thoughts and feelings, encompass the full reality of who they are.

All this applies to YHWH. When we hear this name, or any other that references what we consider sacred, we unavoidably project our own feelings and ideas onto it. Moreover, our feelings and ideas change as our perception of the reality beyond the name grows. That any meaning we give the Beyond involves the projection of our subjective feelings is key. For those who project personal feelings onto YHWH, YHWH is a personal being. For those who project impersonal feelings, the name YHWH may variously point towards transcendence, immanence, presence, absence, creativity, a moral imperative, and so on. Yet YHWH, by whatever name it is identified, remains the reality it is, no matter what we think or feel about it. And that reality is Mystery.

To conclude, it can be said we project our expectations onto YHWH, with the meaning YHWH has for us being a reflection of our expectations. But at the same time we are also reaching out beyond ourselves, without knowing what we are reaching towards. In this sense, YHWH is the mysterious Unknown. Judaism has another name for this: Ein Sof, the Infinite. We each make our own approach to YHWH, the Unknown, the Infinite, the Mystery. Accordingly, I do not offer a definition of YHWH here. While drawing on the personal language of the ancient poets and prophets, I leave each reader free to read the following psalms according to their own perspective, understanding and need.

— Keith Hill, Auckland, August 2019

IN BABYLON

INVOCATION

Yahweh! You are our Lord, you give us
all we are. You hang the heavens over our heads,
steer us with your stars.

The Earth you place beneath our feet,
embrace us in its fold. From the deep you draw
the succour that feeds our fragile souls.

With your power you light the Sun,
make the Moon dilate. You water the world
with your love, renew her cyclic face.

Your knowledge sets the seasons' pulse,
dances on the wind. You sow souls across the
Earth, then wait for which will sing.

Nothing is but what you be, life blossoms
on your breath. You roll our hearts through
the world, make every turn a test.

Before we were you marked our paths,
watched us in the womb. You search our substance
with your love, show us what to learn.

With our works you wring our hearts, bind
us to our lives. From our struggles spark the eyes
which see your subtle signs.

For your secret is buried, Lord, deep
beneath our deeds. You reach into our hidden
parts, draw out your mystery.

You test us to embrace us, Lord, lift
our souls to the heights. With your presence you
would love us, wrap us in robes of light.

So we shall sing your song, Lord, until
you in us are born, and surrendered we stand
on Zion, radiant, transformed.

THE SLAVE REVIEWS HIS SITUATION

Here, in Babylon, forgetting
and forgotten, I die. Bound to the altar,
I feed Baal's devouring fires.

I know our prophets proclaim
Nebuchadnezzar your servant too, yet his being
denies your name, inverting the truth.

"Bow to Baal," he hissed, "learn the
power of my word." Jerusalem refused him—
and suffered his sword.

Gathered, we tried to pray. His soldiers
attacked at dawn. By night, massacred, we were
too shocked to mourn.

Scattered, dismembered, we became
a people enslaved. Shackled, heads shaved,
we seeped through the open gates.

Jerusalem, we sullied you, left your streets
littered with dead. Pools poisoned, offerings
withered, your temple fell to neglect.

Now, each dusk I lament my fate, come
dawn I count the years, but my well has run dry,
I'm a bird trapped in Babylon's snare.

Lord, will I see my home again? Or am
I condemned to this fall? Save me, a slave who
waits weeping for your gathering call!

IN THE TEMPLE OF BAAL

Gongs strike, Baal's priests kneel, their
chanting voices laud. As flames leap skywards,
across cold stones shadows crawl.

Jewelled arms lift. Their robes dazzle.
Eager eyes dilate. To the altar's bound
a virgin: terror tears her face.

Yahweh, your judgement says evil will
have its reward—so why allow these "priests"
to give perversion their applause?

For the virgin was sacrificed, but at
dawn, inside. Wild with wine they clawed her.
Her screams still clutch my mind.

And now I watch them offer this
"virgin" to their god. Is this our promised
future? Then I know I am lost.

Helpless, I have but one choice:
to live or to die. Show your mercy, Lord.
Lift me from Baal's soulless lie!

HIS CAPTORS MAKE A DEMAND

And there I sat, by the waters
of Babylon. I sat and I wept as
I remembered Zion.

Disconsolate, alone, my heart
reached out for death. I hung my harp
on a willow, and I bent my head.

Drunk, they cried, "Sing us a song
of your homeland, sing of how your Lord's
strength helps you command."

And I put my head in my hands.
I made no reply. I hid my face from them
so none could hear me cry.

What do they know? Their breath
stinks of their drunkenness. I could never
sing to you in their vile presence.

My Jerusalem! When I think
of her I shiver. If ever I forget her
may my right hand wither.

Yahweh, you remember how
they laughed at your laws? And how they
spat on Jerusalem's pure walls?

This daughter of Babel's a whore.
Return her mock. Take her! Crush her! Throw
her children screaming on the rock!

Yahweh, you are my Lord. My song
is for you alone. They will never hear me
sing, never of Zion, my home.

THE REALITY OF LIFE IN BABYLON

Give me dove's wings, Lord, to fly
from this despair. In the desert I'd seek refuge,
among wild winds—anywhere!

For all here are drunk. They dance
on twisted knives. Death attends their days,
yet this Babylon calls life.

Above, soldiers' glinting spears spike
the high city walls; below, to distraction,
scream hawkers, lying priests, fools.

No just voices are heard here, none
nurtures the young. And how cruelly Babylon
treats your daughters and sons!

Our suckling babies' tongues cleave to their
mouths from thirst; when our starving children
cry they're struck by handfuls of dirt.

Yahweh, your people are fallen, all
forget their task, their sordid breath is sour,
rottenness eats their hearts.

Those who once ate lawfully today
scrounge in the streets, whom you promised
sanctuary now eat dung and sleep.

I shudder, Lord, to see the doom
that devours this life. Babylon! Beast! May
you fall in your vomit and die!

HE IS PLAGUED BY BABYLON'S PRIESTS

Yahweh! Hear my plea for help.
I pray you heed my cry. In Babylon's pit I rot.
Death gnaws me. I will die.

Yesterday, at dawn, the high priest
stripped his virgins bare. I was forced to wash
their bodies, to comb their matted hair.

"Why not touch them?" his priests
taunted, "Fondle their flesh!" I called on your
name, holding the one hope I have left.

Yet before Baal I tremble. His priests'
words brand me inside. Each night the day's
wounds lie glowing in my mind.

For Babel's soldiers strut the streets,
spitting on us slaves, while her street women
all snigger, "We're a field. Come graze!"

In despair, I searched sixty inns,
seeking just one friend. From face to face
I looked: vacant eyes just stared.

I saw that no slave knows, Lord,
the prayer you placed in man, nor the faith you
foster, the hope nurtured by your hands.

And now my life wilts, Lord,
in the face of all that craves. Lost, cast down,
may your love lift me from this pain!

THE SLAVE SIGHS FOR HIS BELOVED

Last night, on my bed, I sought you whom
my heart loves. In the moonlight, insensible,
my heart suffused with blood.

My beloved, you know you are
my only lover. I remember you, for our Lord
gave us to one another.

When I lost you in the desert march,
yes, I wept. My eyes blurred and I stumbled.
My fractured feet bled.

So it was, last night, that desolation
swept my heart. Once again I felt the anguish
of our being far apart.

I rose and walked, I sang to the moon
in the sky. The night watchmen started:
I soothed them with a sigh.

Longing, inspired, I flew high above
Babylon's streets. I glimpsed a wadi where
sky and horizon meet.

And I thought, there! That is where
my beloved waits! That is the rendezvous
to which I must escape!

Then I sank down onto my bed,
overcome with bliss. And I dreamed, wonderful!
I dreamed I felt your kiss.

HE IS AWAKENED BY A DREAM

I stirred. The patriarch's presence
drenched me with fear. The command in his
eyes was more than I could bear.

I felt him touch my heart, probe
my inner core, and in my most hidden place
something secret tore.

Shame flooded me, I perceived
the worst I am. And I tried to hide from what
saw I was not a man.

Then, in silence within, Abraham
said, "Be still." And I was drained of fear
by something beyond my will.

I melted; not in peace, but knowing
I was seen, for he felt my ache, the flight
that fills my dreams.

"What you want," he said, "you must
seek among the wise. Yet they are hidden,
for each wears a disguise."

Then Abraham left. Awe-struck,
trembling, I awoke. I lit incense, my prayers
ascended with the smoke.

I praised you then, Lord, and I'm
full of awe now. Upright in your wisdom,
I can only bend in a low bow.

THE SLAVE MEETS DANIEL

He entered the square at noon,
his eyes flashed of the sun. I was praying
and sweeping, my shirt all undone.

He commanded, "Follow," and led me
into the streets. We walked from the market,
sat after washing our feet.

I declared my pain; he praised the heart's
subtle movement. My thrilled mind jumped:
could this be the great secret?

He smiled and stilled me, silence entered
as thought fell, and for the first time I saw
my own pain locks me in this hell.

Then, in the market glare, I considered
my fellow exiles, how so few remember their
home, how none wish to be wise.

I said, "Yahweh is disappointed with
the sons of men." He said, "Yahweh seeks
those who seek Jerusalem."

I said, "They claim Yahweh's contracted
with their blood." He said, "Each must find
his own peace with what is above."

I said, "When I speak of lack, they just
say I'm crazed. They believe the Book tells
them they're already saved."

He said, "Baal reaches right through
their temple's walls. Complete your duty, but
keep inner and outer divorced.

"Work with the one soul you have
the power to perfect: you will illuminate others
as light in you collects."

DOUBT STILL TORMENTS THE SLAVE

I am confused, Lord, doubts
darken my mind. Beneath me my feet falter,
above is a reeling sky.

For you forgive our errors, answer
our emptiness, your awful judgement promises
to punish injustice.

Then why do Babylon's cattle fatten,
her full tables groan, while your own people
starve and forget their kin and home?

You call on us, your chosen, to make
a straight way for you, yet here crookedness
prospers and the upright are pursued.

Lord, I accept your word, that your
law is true and just. I believe you'll restore
wisdom by building on our trust.

But my heart is troubled, to my mind
little makes sense. Show me a sign, let me see
the working of your intent.

Yahweh, I have faith, but in this world
I doubt myself. Brutalized, fragmented, tender
this slave your help!

HE PERCEIVES THE NATURE OF THE WORLD

I fall asleep, I die, I plummet through
the dreams of men. I wake, I live, yet seeing
the world who would not die again?

For nation devours nation, whole peoples
suffer for gain: kings kill, courtiers count, priests
justify what their gods profane.

All wealth flows to Babylon, all power,
knowledge, pride. Her people suck on plunder,
her leaders propound lies.

Each day Babylon's soldiers guard mute
gods made of gold. Their words, pronounced
by priests, enthral empty souls.

Babylon's wealthy are blind, they dress
in bones for Baal. Her usurers honored, dissenters
line the streets, impaled.

This is Baal's sorcery: those who have
worship wealth's cold laws, while death crawls
from the desert to devour Babylon's poor.

Lord, I live in a land of ghosts,
all are equally cursed: owner or owned,
each occupies a house disturbed.

All this that pours into us sends shivers
through our dreams. Wake us, Lord, that your life,
through us, may be redeemed.

THE SLAVE CONSIDERS HIS HERITAGE

In my father's house I stand, hearing
his firm steps. My mother's song caresses,
her milk sweet on my lips.

How lovely on the mountain slopes
floated her soft feet, walking where gazelles graze,
filling the garden with peace.

My parents still feed me now, their
pulse fills my life: their love is my garden,
their guidance my delight

And I still carry, in my acts, the weight
of their words, for their fathers spoke through
them, building me from birth.

The foundations are the law; walls,
teachings from the past; windows, my application;
roof, rituals to bind us fast.

When Babel's soldiers broke the doors I lost
more than my self: the winepress of tradition
broke, my house of heritage fell.

And now I mourn, today, the children
of Abraham; yet I vow to walk backwards until
I reclaim what I am.

May I not stumble, Lord, nor drop
your precious key, 'til I have rebuilt, from
the cornerstone, Zion's sanctuary.

HE HEARS A VOICE CALLING HIM

Stock still in the street I halt, heart
held in my hand. Yet what have I to offer?
What do I truly know? Or understand?

Lord, I am not what you made, not what I
yet could be. Though I daily stride the streets,
insignificance fills my deeds.

At noon I stand in darkness, at dusk captivity
spreads its cold. My blanket's made of maggots,
no knowledge nightly soaks my soul.

Yet that is when I hear it, a call that
penetrates my chest: in a beat I pause, a still
point in Babylon's reeling unrest.

How far, this call asks, will I
allow my life to fall? Yet how can I change?
I am a numberless slave, no more.

Each day I'm commanded, by voices
harsh yet dumb. They've made me hate my life;
no, hate what I've become.

I am but a casket of attitudes,
an accident of bones. Should soldiers kill me
today who would care I was gone?

I eat the bread of suffering, drink
the water of distress. Your call cries inside me,
Lord, but what I am remains unsaid.

DANIEL TEACHES THE WAY TO ESCAPE

All day I sat brooding, sorrows
haunted my mind. Daniel approached; gently,
he merged his heart with mine.

Silent, we meditated, high above
the streets. Below the mobs caroused;
within, my heart knew peace.

When the sun sank he lit the
tapers on the wall. "Wakefulness," he said,
"is the first commandment of the Lord.

"For none who slept ever escaped
from Babylon. Whatever their hopes, they died
drinking the tavern's song."

"How then," I asked, "when taverns
guard the five gates out?" "Not that way,"
he said, "but inside the city itself.

"At Babylon's center stands a
hidden well. Above it is a tunnel to
bring you from your hell.

"But you must want it more than you
want yourself, for death will take you if for
a moment you doubt."

"I want it more than the dead
long for light." My heart leaps, Lord,
for now I'll discover life!

A DREAM CAUSES WONDER AND CONFUSION

I bow my head, Lord, in your dawn
light unmasked, for last night a puzzling
vision entered my heart.

Through a valley I walked, beside
a cooling stream. Sipping at blossoms, I saw
bright-feathered birds feed.

From the earth's huge depths, a clear,
pure spring bubbled; concealed in the trees
rare plants drank its waters.

Then, dwarfed by the growth, I saw
a strange tree's shoots: roots above the earth,
it was hung with perfect fruit.

To this I was drawn, as a bee to
a perfect flower; yet, while I watched, the tree
transformed into my lover.

Gorgeous, draped with light, unmoving
she reached to me, but I held back, for this
was someone I had never seen.

I started awake then, wondering
at what I saw, so aware she both was and
was not with me in the dawn.

Yet, as the sun rose, I vowed to open
to her my breast, and live for her presence:
her warmth, her perfume, her breath.

THE SLAVE ESCAPES FROM BABYLON

That day, for the last time, I was
Baal's temple drudge. I did my duty with
the bodies, washed away the blood.

But when the next watch replaced me
I slipped past the guards. Through the back
streets I ran, hope as high as the stars.

No one walked the market, it was
silent, empty, cold. Above burned the moon,
its light terrible and old.

And in that vast stillness I said
a small, grateful prayer: others had been before
me, their efforts had helped me here.

Then I unwound the rope Daniel
had bid me make. I approached the well,
tied it, lowered myself, and escaped.

A tunnel waited, as Daniel said,
just above the water. I slid in, pulled down
the rope, used its ends as a taper.

For the wall held a torch, perpetually
burning in oil: lit by the burning rope
I continued that night's toil.

My steps were towards salvation,
with each one I prayed. Odd shouts rang out.
I ignored them. All stank of the grave.

Until, at last, from a cave I emerged
to continue my quest. Behind stood Babylon,
before the wilderness.

And there too was Daniel; my mind
leaped in surprise. "I'm not of Babylon," he said,
and gave me my disguise.

I am to be a shepherd, guiding
Babylon's flocks. "None will look for you thus."
I changed among the rocks.

IN THE WILDERNESS

THE SONG OF THE GOOD SHEPHERD

I paused. Yahweh, I waited for you
to hear my cry. And you heard! You stooped
down from the sky!

You lifted me from the pit where
in clay I slipped and turned. You set my feet on
the rock and made my footsteps firm.

Now a new song fills me, Lord, my
freed heart sings. Throat and tongue cry out,
making the wilderness ring.

The night owl hears me, it looks from
its nest and hoots. The sheep stare at this
madman. The goats stop chewing shoots.

Through these vast, rocky spaces my
voice strides out, dies. The stars, approving,
ripple. Truly, I feel inspired!

So many wonders have you for your
people performed. No hand matches yours.
None else deserves the name Lord.

You spoke to Moses from fire, turned
Aaron's rod into a snake. Water you sprang from
stone that our thirst might be slaked.

And now, for me tonight, you have
again worked your will. Where before I felt
assaulted, now I am still.

Dawn stains the sky; as a shepherd I
am now blessed. My Lord, how can I thank you?
I am lifted out of death!

THE WORK OF THE GOOD SHEPHERD

Into the wilderness I led my sheep
and goats forth. As the dogs barked I
remembered what I had been taught.

"The sun is now your guide"—such
was Daniel's instruction. "Where it sets,
that is Jerusalem's direction."

So saying, he had shown me
three dogs and a crook. "Use your eyes
to hear, feet to feel, ears to look.

"For the good shepherd is ever
awake and alert. He knows all sources
of danger, the wiles of the earth.

"When the wind rises, he gives his
flock safe shelter. He knows thorny from
lush grass, good from bad water.

"The dogs too must become
your obedient limbs, for now they wander,
fight, are lazy, lack discipline.

"A poor shepherd reveals a slave
trying to hide. Babylon's men will find
and unmask him: he will die.

"To reach Jerusalem, you must
change yourself, for without being what
you seem your west will turn south.

"Thus remain ever watchful, both
without and within. Let your crook guide the flock.
That way you will not return."

And with these guiding words, he left
me to my task. Now I stride though the dust,
happiness in my heart.

Lord, such ecstasy now fills me
I could sing down the sky. What more can I say?
I'm privileged to be alive!

THE REALITY OF LIFE IN THE WILDERNESS

Yahweh, my Lord! Why have you
forsaken me? Day and night for weeks I've called.
Your silence is deafening.

Where am I? I am lost. My feet
are not my own. My heart has gone dry.
My dull prayers stumble on stones.

Neither the dogs obey my voice, nor
the flock my crook. When I bring them all
to water in it float dead rooks.

And the desert people—I've not met
their like before. "A worm you are," they shriek
at me, "not a man at all!"

They unleashed their dogs. Flesh hangs
now from my hands and feet. They even stole
my new robe: I'm wearing dirty sheets.

Finally in the rocks I fell, bleeding
in the sun. Now each of my bones aches.
I can count every one.

Yahweh, where's my fault? Have I
disobeyed your law? Then why is my heart
melted, tongue stuck to my jaw?

Life is meant to make sense. I
understand nothing. I was on my way home,
but I've found only suffering.

My beloved waits, somewhere
beyond the horizon. Make me worthy of her,
Lord, for I have become poison!

SOLDIERS FIND THE SHEPHERD

Today I found an oasis. There I
watered my flock. But standing still,
drinking, I suffered a great shock.

The dogs began growling, my hackles
stiffened in alarm, then five soldiers emerged
from behind a clump of palms.

"Slave!" one screamed abruptly. "We know
you've escaped!" Two grabbed my arms, a third
sneered, a fourth spat in my face.

Then the fifth struck and kicked
me, threw me into the dust—that moment
I learned of the just and unjust.

For I stood straight up, saying, "This
is Baal's priest's flock. If one dies through
neglect, it will be at your lives' cost."

They stepped back doubtfully: this
was not how slaves act. One grabbed my
gourd, tasted, spat and threw it back.

"Bitter!" he cried. "Only a true slave
could drink this!" As they walked away,
laughing, I gave my luck a kiss.

Yahweh, luck saved me because
you taught me strength. Through being
neglected I've learned to act and think.

Now I understand: we're purified
by such tests. It won't be long, beloved.
I am on my way west!

PRAISE FOR YAHWEH, GOAL AND GUIDE

Yahweh, you guide me, your light
illuminates my path. My heart is in your
stronghold, my mind to you bound fast.

My enemies drew near, seeking
to consume my flesh, but it was they who
stumbled, they who slipped towards death.

Though an army besiege me, still
my heart won't fear; though war engulf me,
my mind will hold you near.

For one goal only do I struggle
through this strife: to live in your house,
Lord, all the days of my life.

When malice stalks, you give me
refuge in your tent. On your rock you
sit me, safe from evil intent.

And now my head is lifted
above my enemies: this joy I sacrifice
for escaping their enmity.

"Seek my face," you say. Lord, you
know that is my task. So do not hide yourself,
teach me to walk your path.

I will always walk, Lord, towards
the land of the living, for it's birth, not death,
those on your path are given!

HE PONDERS THE IMPONDERABLE

Day dies, night comes, through
the sky constellations wheel. Lying beneath them,
I wonder what their patterns reveal.

For who knows his destiny, what fate
has in store? Unseen is tomorrow, unknown
the workings of the law.

I was free, then fell; now I walk
the wilderness. That I would become a shepherd
who would ever have guessed?

Hidden influences play down
into our lives. One walks west, one east:
the reason baffles the mind.

Lord, you plant great longing deep
in each person's breast. But few feel it, few make
its unravelling their life's quest.

And those who do seek you, how many
live your way? Too few argue the skeletons
the singing sands have betrayed.

Yahweh, beneath your sky I feel
life's mystery. Whatever I am, Lord, help me
to fulfil my destiny!

HE IS A CRY IN THE WILDERNESS

Deliver me, my Lord, my life is
in your hands. Lift me out of myself,
into your promised land.

My days disperse like smoke, my skin
has become stone. Blistered by the desert sun,
the flesh burns from my bones.

Each day I drive my flock through
a heat haze of dirt. When night falls I don't
sleep, but brood like a lonely bird.

My works wither, my thoughts
are a violent rash. My daily bread I choke on,
its taste tear-stained ash.

Like a mad pelican, I am caught
in my own nest. With the wild camels
I wreck the wilderness.

And Baal's soldiers still track me: night's
filled with their eyes. Their lying lips whisper,
Lord, that you don't love my life!

Yet I'll seek you, though the skin
sear from my back, for without such a search
this body's an empty sack.

Under a savage sun, Yahweh, I still
hold your name. Know I'll always walk your
path, though withered, haunted, lame.

HE REACHES THE WADI HE DREAMED OF

Through the heat haze it rose, a gift
from above. As I spied its distant shimmer
my heart lifted in love.

Prayers sang through me as I strode across
the sand. The flock, smelling water, surged too.
I stayed them, crook in hand.

Yet surprise soon snared me.
Merchants filled every way. Some, ecstatic, sang.
Under palms stood others, dazed.

And as my flock and dogs drank
I discovered why: so divine that water tasted
a shiver straightened my spine!

For all here possessed mysteries, not one
was mundane: healers, psychics, magicians,
from each face powers flamed.

And I too, from those waters, now
felt immensely strong. Single-handed, I knew,
I could even smash Babylon!

Then a passing stranger caught
my ear with his mind. Silent he was, yet
spoke with Daniel's command.

"Beware of the idols," he warned,
"which all here embrace, for in the body's
temple each worships his own face."

He vanished. Chastised, I paused
and saw I was alone, for under the wadi's
palms all had made permanent home.

Each was a potent master, each saw
himself as saved. I called my dogs, herded
the flock, sadly turned away.

So many traps, Lord, entice those
who hear your call, but to come so far then
halt: it seems to mock your law.

Yet, don't doubt me, Yahweh, my steps
shall never divert. For whatever your gifts,
only you can quench my thirst!

THE SHEPHERD REUNITES WITH HIS LOVER

That night, in my tent, my existence
was transformed. From the darkness stepped
she for whom I was born.

Her feet, with myrrh anointed, walked
without a sound. Her tender eyes grazed mine
as, gently, she sat down.

A mystery she was, more serene
than moonrise: I bathed in her beauty, then
fell into her eyes.

How long did we sit and gaze as
breezes stroked our hair? Did we sit at all?
Or did we rather float on air?

My heart, my soul, my love, we said what
no lip speaks, then, when those lips touched,
fountains flowered in the deep.

Wine and spices flowed from our hearts
across our tongues. Ecstatic, our clothes fell:
naked, two became one.

And there, among the stars, sailed a
single rhapsodic cry. Living, but dead,
in bliss we both expired.

My love! In your presence I found
what life truly means: your eyes, your touch,
your laugh—all else is merely dream.

THE SHEPHERD'S SHEPHERD

You are our shepherd, Yahweh, we
shall never want. To still waters you lead us,
to sip their sacred font.

Restored, calm, into us descends
your subtle flow. On sweet grasses you lay us,
then we know, we know!

Though we walked the valley
of death we did never fear, for your name
soothed us, keeping shelter near.

Now you fill us, Lord, with your
presence are we taught. Your rod and staff
in us, we need no other support.

Your table you offer us, despite
our enemies' dread. Your cup you make us,
with oil anoint our head.

Good, grace, and mercy are present
each of our days. Your house we enter when
we remember why we were made.

Yahweh, the good in our life wholly
comes from you. May the task you've set us,
we do, and do, and do!

THE SHEPHERD AND HIS BELOVED RESUME

At dawn we left the wadi while
those who lived there slept. Jerusalem beckoned.
We continued our wilderness trek.

Yet the paths were diverse, as many
had journeyed here. The waymarks all had fallen.
My mind began to fear.

For Jerusalem was far, the chance
of error great, and strayed from the path
we would share the dumb beasts' fate.

Then my beloved soothed me:
"Yahweh knows the way." Abruptly I awoke:
thoughts had my heart betrayed.

You give us your gifts, Lord,
to guide us on your path; in truth you help us
walk, bring love into our hearts.

You save the upright, the good, by
teaching them your law. The wayward feet you
rescue of the humble and the poor.

Know I shall do what my heart loves,
avoid what it hates, for my heart holds fast to you,
in it resides my faith.

Lord, to Jerusalem bring us, by your
blessed hand, and there make us fruitful
that our seed inherit your land.

ON THE BANKS OF THE JORDAN

It snaked through the wilderness.
We stood still and gasped. The blinding sun it
reflected. We bent our knees and basked.

And as we knelt in silence, the sleek
waters swelled: a lion leaped from the surge
to where the strongest dwell.

It clawed us like a whirlwind,
biting us inside. Powerful, devouring, it
straightened up our spine.

Then, with one graceful bound,
it leaped over our head. The roar fell, the waters
dipped, we slumped as if dead.

Yahweh, from dust you formed us,
breathed into our mouth, laid out your endless
plain that yawns from north to south.

Spent people have you put here,
devouring all they find, of cruelty building
homes, with madness in their eyes.

Lord, avoiding these ungodly,
we fight stones and thorns; thirst-bent, half
mad ourselves, yet longing to be yours.

And now beside the Jordan, we stand
in lush cypress groves. Grateful we collapse,
yet frightened by what we know.

For in your hidden places secrets
are laid bare; here you reward the struggles
of those who have dared.

Yet the pit is present also, waiting
one false move: give us what we need, Lord,
not what desire approves.

Yahweh, your glory springs from
this carcass of clay. You made it, it is yours,
do with it what you may.

YAHWEH'S GIFT OF WISDOM

In the night rain falls. That dawn
desert flowers open. Through vibrant
blossoms the little lizards slither.

Behind, the bloomed desert, before
us foothill tracks ascend. Subtly clothed in
blessings, we climb towards Jerusalem.

Then the sound of footsteps echoes
high in the trees. From the leaf litter steps
Daniel, peaceful and serene.

Surprise unravels my thoughts.
I stop with a start. Discerning my state,
my beloved and Daniel both laugh.

"I am where you are," says Daniel,
and takes me aside. Under the sun we sit:
his teaching settles my mind.

"In the beginning," he says, "Yahweh
unfolded his purpose. He first created Wisdom,
then his worldly works.

"Before the deep gushed, mountains
settled, Wisdom was born. Before the world
existed she formed the throne of the Lord.

"With Yahweh she sat when
he caused the world to be. Into his design
she impressed her subtle seed.

"Ever playful, she gave the Lord
perpetual delight: into the habitable she
leapt that hearts not remain blind.

"Thus there is one teaching for those
who would be wise: learn to know that
which is not from the outside.

"For that is Wisdom, her light dwells
deep in you. Your beloved your guide,
through her love be illumed."

THE SHEPHERD APPRECIATES HIS BELOVED

I turn to my beloved, our eyes
gently kiss, and in the silence I come
to know what she is.

My darling, you are the ointment
to heal my arid heart: your love pours over
me, soothing my ancient scars.

Your scent is of cedars, your lips
secrete wine, and you are fair, my love,
your beauty stills my mind.

Love, come lie with me, scatter
myrrh across our bed: while outside the tent
kids skitter, within we shall ascend.

Let intoxicating kisses cascade
from your mouth, in their honeyed comfort
may I forget myself.

For you are fair, my love, fairer
than the cooing doves, gentler than the dew
that nightly falls from above.

All my years I have wondered if
I sought too much; now between your breasts
I lie, loving your tender touch.

In you shall I surrender the
action of my life, for you are fair my love,
a fragrance from paradise.

YAHWEH, THE SOLE REFUGE

As deer scour the mountains, seeking
bubbling streams, so I long for you, Yahweh,
who are everything I mean.

As lizards in the sun lie, that their
cold skin may warm, so in your light I live
Lord, whether dusk or dawn.

When birds each morning sing, all
spirits are renewed; when night wraps the world
in sleep those spirits sail to you.

Fruit from the tree hangs, so do
we on you depend: if we should seed or rot
it's you decides our end.

The snake on the earth crawls, your
judgement struck it down, yet should you bid
it stand its legs are then unbound.

Your word sustains the world, speak
and it is done; leaves wilt, tight blossoms bloom,
your measure rules the sun.

Like meadow flowers in spring, Lord,
we are but your guests, for every breath we take
you breathe into our chests.

Time itself in you stands, like a leaf
paused on the wind, but as worms in dust writhe
so we fall to childish whims.

This whole entrancing world is but
the echo of your voice: eat the echo, seek
the source, such is ever our choice.

As the deer lows at dawn,
longing for its mate, so I long for you, Lord:
may I one day know your face!

THEY SEE THE WALLS OF JERUSALEM

From the mist it emerged, gates
glistening in the dew. From mountains set like
footstools rose pillars lit by the moon.

Walls made of glowing silver,
it shimmered in the night, while through
its foundations a radiant river twined.

Jerusalem! We left divided, weeping,
but return wrapped in song. Eyes raised, united,
we remember the mystery of Zion.

Fill our mouths with laughter, Lord,
pour into us your joy, create in us your stillness,
that what we are uncoils.

Across the plains you pulled us when
doubt delayed our course; each night your silence
loved us, dissolving us to our core.

And now we watch in wonder as
clouds clear from the peaks, and sublime, soaring,
Jerusalem swells in the west.

Our lips praise only you, Yahweh,
in whose presence we abide, for we're here because
you opened, not because we arrived.

IN JERUSALEM

THE LOVERS ENTER JERUSALEM

Here stand Jerusalem's gates. Here lies
your promised land. Here heaven is distilled,
makes drunk the little lambs.

Happiness floods my heart. From
the sky honey falls. Love lifts my face—
then my foot hits a donkey pat.

I strike earth; my mouth tastes dirt;
filth stings my eyes. Daniel's words reveal
the excrement in my mind.

"Fool!" he chides. "Don't lead, become
a servant and obey. Follow your beloved.
Let her presence dissolve your shame."

He leaves. She reaches out. Her kiss
suffuses my heart as, gently, she lifts me
into the sky's glowing arch.

On love's ladder we rise, over plains
and limpid lakes; Zion's peak we approach,
its snow reflected in her face.

And deep in her eyes I perceive
the progress of my life: in the stations of
my years I read wisdom's subtle signs.

Jerusalem's gates open, revealing
our sacred home, and we are beckoned
within, to blossom in what we know.

THE KNOWING SERVANT'S SONG

Yahweh, you created us, from dust
you formed our frame. So we might stand upright,
you straightened us with your name.

Storms shall not swallow our faith,
nor fires scorch our mind, for you are our source,
Lord, on you we stand our lives.

You carved a way through the desert,
quenched our driving thirst; wild beasts you knelt
before us to show the power of your works.

Now your feet walk the mountains, gates
open to your touch, and the watchmen all wait
silent for the mystery of your love.

Once we were Babylon's slaves, our
humanity ignored: infested, sores dripping,
people ran from us, appalled.

Then, men of sorrows, we entered
the wilderness: our souls caught fire, blistered,
of all possessions stripped.

But like spring saplings we survived
the desert heat, and now, restored through poverty,
we blossom in your peace.

Lord, you said we would prosper, be exalted
to great heights, but we're content to serve you,
to discern your subtle signs.

The old world dissolved, you build
new heaven, new earth: from flames fanned
by your hands comes Zion's hidden birth.

Doubt now is fallen, salvation drapes
us in its robes, and life in us rises, Lord,
as your splendour you bestow.

FIRST SONG OF THE BELOVED

I am dark, but comely, like the tents that
drape Kedar, for the desert sun consumed me
as I watched men from afar.

In my bed each night I sang my
naked song: "Who has seen my love," I sighed,
"he for whom I long?"

Then leaping over hills you came,
bounding through dawn mist! Look where you
stood at the wall, peering through the lattice!

Now I am the rose of Sharon,
the lily of the valley. As an apple tree in
the woods, so is your love to me.

You brought me to your banquet,
your wine my sorrow quenched, with apples you
restored me, your raisins fed my strength.

And now I am sick with love,
your face invades my heart. Like a dove I hide in
the cliffs, then swoop into your arms.

Yes, I shall sip the lips of you
whom I adore, for you are my beloved,
and I, my love, am yours!

THE SERVANT WEDS HIS BELOVED

From above swoops the spirit. Flowers
sprout across the land. Mountains spring like
lions, the hills like frisking lambs.

In the garden our eyes open as, on
us, blessings pour. Heads bowed, grateful,
we gather the gifts of our Lord.

And from their midst steps you,
gorgeous, glowing, serene. In the love your
face radiates, my existence is redeemed.

You allure in your wedding dress,
blooms adorn your hair. Join me at the altar,
for your virtues brought me here.

All I am I give to you, my desires,
my future, my beliefs. I surrender to your
presence, for your touch sings of peace.

The days of my life lead here, to you
who makes me whole. From the seeds our love
scatters may a new life now evolve.

Returned, raised up, on unity's
ladder we climb, for I am your beloved,
and you, my bride, are mine.

SECOND SONG OF THE BELOVED

Lift your face, my love, embrace
this song of songs. The turtle dove is cooing,
the winter rains have gone.

I'll take you to my house, we'll
spend the night in wine. At dawn we'll join
the birds that flit among the vines.

We'll watch the blossoms open,
the pomegranates bloom. We'll cut rare fruits
from mandrake roots, traditional and new.

And we'll chase the little foxes, their
grinning snouts so sly. With them we'll chew
the flowers, make havoc in the vines.

Then we'll enter my father's house
where he will show his love: for you he'll pour
spiced wine, served in Wisdom's cup.

Come lie with me, my love, make
the soft flowers a couch; delight my neck and
cheeks with kisses from your mouth.

Place your left hand under my head,
right upon my breast, and let us never stir,
for together we are blessed.

THE REALITY OF LIFE IN JERUSALEM

Grant us wisdom, Yahweh, make us
consorts to your throne. May we there surrender
what we are to be in Zion reborn.

In the desert we gathered, collecting
your gifts in our hands: hope, to feed our future,
discipline, to understand.

And now at your instruction we build
an altar on your peak, an image of the beginning
in which your word may speak.

To there descends, in darkness,
Wisdom on your breath: we pass her our powers,
she erects your house of rest.

Through her radiates truth; truth
generates your law; your law we hear and obey;
practice makes us pure and poor.

In poverty we find ourselves, the source
of what we be; to being comes a robe of light
allotted from your canopy.

Our efforts come to nothing, Yahweh,
but what you in us do give, for our struggle lights
the path, but by your birth we live.

THE UNITY OF LOVER AND BELOVED

We took off our tunics and washed
our rested feet. With the first drops of dew
we felt moonlight from the east.

Night bloomed, we slept, but our hearts
watched in our chests. Soon the garden filled with
perfume, prompting us to forget.

Awake, you winds of Lebanon, stir
the lions in their lair: loose the mountain leopards
to search the vineyards of Senir.

Branches shook, I tensed, my beloved
soothed my brow. "It's a breeze," she whispered,
and loosed our undergowns.

My beloved bathes in lilies whose scent
redoles of bliss; to the ardour rising in me
she bared her fragrant breasts.

The gate rattled. I started. In fear
my fervor froze. "It's the dark," she said.
From her sweet tongue nectar flowed.

Blow, winds of Lebanon, shed your secrets
where you will; from Hermon's sacred heights
release the wine your peace distils.

The trees trembled. The lock dissolved.
He stepped through the door. "It's the mystery,"
she sighed—we shuddered to our core.

I pray, you daughters of Zion, do not
disturb my love, for by the desert gazelles,
I swear, her eyes are full of doves.

And drench in myrrh, you wild winds,
our bent heads and hands, as in silence we soar
out of ourselves, across the promised land.

EVOCATION

In the beginning you were, Lord, before
what was to be. From you came the mountains,
the plains and shifting seas.

In you the welling world dwells, cupped
in both your hands, for you are our source, Lord,
in us your silence stands.

From dry dust you shaped us, put
your pulse into our acts: to dust we shall dissolve
if we fail to fill our lack.

On each single second depends
the judgement you dispense, yet all the world's
time, Lord, is a moment on your breath.

When your anger flares, forests
wither, whirlwinds rake: driving on the storm
your wrath crushes all you hate.

Yet the tender rain that quenches is
your requiting touch: the desert bloom, the fecund
fig, show your transforming love.

Your grace flows through us, giving life
to senseless clay, our troubles fevered dreams
you gently brush away.

All our secrets you see, Lord,
trembling in your sight, for you know all we
do, transcendent in the heights.

Teach us to count our days, Lord, let
wisdom swell our hearts; may we be each morning
grateful we've woken from the dark.

Let your servants show, Lord, what they
can do for you, and may your glory ignite us,
transparent so you shine through.

THE MYSTIC TASK OF REINTEGRATION

The journey from Babylon to Jerusalem is one of reintegration, in which seekers gather the dissociated parts of their psyche and re-arrange them into a new unity. Last century a number of philosophic and psychospiritual approaches were developed to encourage this process.

Existential philosophers focused on humanity's inhumanity towards others. They concluded that destructive behaviour resulted from a state of dissociation, in which people surrendered their personal volition to destructive political, philosophic and social programmes. They considered this inhumanity would only be overcome when individuals stopped living in bad faith and by becoming true to their deep selves, rather than adhering to a socially constructed doctrine or idealogy. Then they would start living authentically.

Jungian psychology offered a more detailed analysis, identifying diverse aspects of the psyche: the personal unconscious, anima and animus (female and male drives), the shadow self and its complexes, introverted and extroverted attitudes, and archetypes present deep in the collective unconscious. Integration for Jung involved drawing together the psyche's various, often conflicting, parts into a reintegrated and harmonious whole.

Transpersonal psychology, linked to the human potential movement founded in Esalen, California, in the 1960s, explored heightened states of awareness and their contribution to spiritual development. Similar to Jung's goal of transforming the individual, the transpersonal movement sought to harmonise the spiritual with the everyday and thereby forge a new, integrated lifestyle and identity.

In Judaism, the process of harmonising is called tikkun olam. It involves deep healing, in which individuals strive to re-balance and heal not just themselves but also the world, on all levels: material, moral, political, psychological and spiritual.

Returning from inner exile and reintegrating our psyche is a complex task. People vary in their social backgrounds, cultural upbringing, experiences and outlook, so have different issues they need to address. In the following I will focus on the psyche's re-integration from a spiritual perspective. But before doing so, I need to discuss the interlinked spiritual and literary influences that shaped the poems in this collection, as they laid the foundations for the approach I have adopted.

THE PSALMS' MAIN THREE SOURCES

For this psalm sequence, three ancient Hebrew texts have principally been drawn on: the *Psalms*, *The Song of Songs* and *Isaiah*. These are supplemented by St John of the Cross' *Spiritual Canticle*, itself a mystical response to *The Song of Songs*, and two works of Islamic Sufism: Farid ud-Din Attar's thirteenth century poem, *Manteq at-Tair (Conference of the Birds)* and Muhyiddin Ibn 'Arabi's *Turjumân al-Ashwâq (The Interpreter of Desire)*.

The Abrahamic religions—Judaism, Christianity and Islam—not only draw on the same inspirational texts written by the ancient Jewish prophets and poets, each worships the same Deity, Abraham's God, Accordingly, their mystic traditions are intertwined, and they expound similar metaphysical themes and practices. In the discussion of integration that follows, I will consider the process of inner integration using the language and imagery of the ancient Jewish prophets and poets, as interpreted by those who worked within the mystical traditions of Judaism, Christianity and Islam. I'll begin with a consideration of *The Song of Songs*.

RABBINIC INTERPRETATIONS OF THE SONG OF SONGS

Sensuous love poetry was written in Sumaria and Egypt at least a millennia before *The Song of Songs* was edited into its current form. Analysis of the *Songs*' vocabulary suggests the editing most likely occurred during the post-Exilic era, in the third century BCE. There is insufficient evidence for us to know whether the editor stitched together existing lyrics, created new songs, or undertook a weaving of both. The *Songs*' editor was likely influenced by Greek literary practice as well as by Sumarian and Egyptian models. The entire region was conquered by Alexander the Great's army in 332 BCE, and scholars have noted the similarity between the pastoral poems of Theocritus, a Greek poet who lived in Alexandria, Egypt, and the *Songs*' pastoral imagery.[1]

The Song of Songs has had a surprisingly long-lasting impact on Western culture; surprising, because the poem's erotic content challenged religious authorities, who are more comfortable with dogmatic, metaphysical and moral materials than the overtly sensual. In Judaism, the *Songs*' erotic content—most of the poems are written from a young woman's perspective, recounting her sexual awakening—led orthodox rabbis to reject the *Songs* as not worthy of inclusion in the Jewish canon. However, by the first century *The Song of Songs* had been ascribed to King Solomon, which protected it from criticism and ensured its status within the canon.

In contrast to orthodox ambivalence, Jewish mystics enthusiastically embraced *The Song of Songs*. In *The Bihar*, a first century mystic work, Rabbi Yochanan is reported to have stated: "All Scripture is holy, and all the Torah is holy, but *The Song of Songs* is the Holy of the Holies. What is the meaning of the Holy of Holies? It means that it is holy for the Holy Ones. What are the Holy Ones? They are the counterparts of the six directions that are in man. That which is holy for them is holy for everything."

Aryeh Kaplan, a twentieth century expositor, explains this somewhat opaque text thus: "While outwardly *The Song of Songs* is simply a beautiful love song, it actually is the most profound song of unification of Zer Anpin [the spiritually developed per-

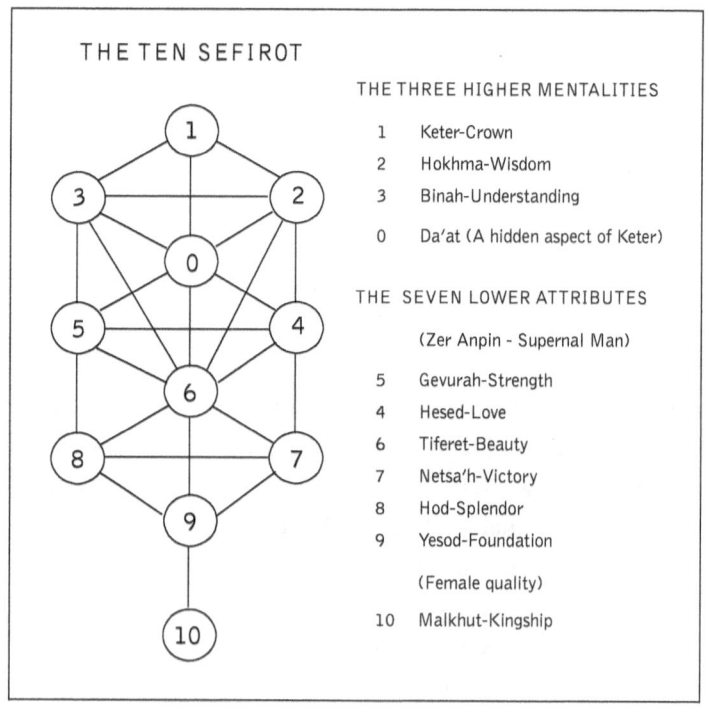

THE TEN SEFIROT

THE THREE HIGHER MENTALITIES

1   Keter-Crown
2   Hokhma-Wisdom
3   Binah-Understanding
0   Da'at (A hidden aspect of Keter)

THE SEVEN LOWER ATTRIBUTES

    (Zer Anpin - Supernal Man)
5   Gevurah-Strength
4   Hesed-Love
6   Tiferet-Beauty
7   Netsa'h-Victory
8   Hod-Splendor
9   Yesod-Foundation

    (Female quality)
10 Malkhut-Kingship

son] and his bride. ... The word holy, in general, indicates separation from the mundane world, and it is insofar as they are transcendental that the Sefirot [the six hidden male spiritual essences of Zer Anpin, which are the six directions to which Rabbi Yochanan referred] are called holy. Similarly, when a person enters into a mystical state, he is said to enter the realm of the 'Holies', that is, of the Sefirot."[2]

These are allegorical readings. Allegory was invented by the Greeks around 500 BCE as they sought to counter the way that Homer, in his great national poems *The Illiad* and *The Odyssey*, had depicted the gods as capricious, self-interested, savage and immoral. This offended the refined sensibilities of fifth century Greeks, who considered they had risen above such primitive notions. Applying an allegorical interpretation allowed them to view Homer's depiction of the gods' lust and killing as something else entirely. For example, according to the allegorisers, when the two gods Apollo and Neptune fought an aerial battle, Homer wasn't describing fighting between two gods but was referring to the mixing of wet (Neptune) and hot (Apollo) elements, which produced thunder and lightning. Over time ever more elaborate allegorical interpretations were conjured, with the gods being considered to alternatively represent planets, astrological signs, moral characteristics and bodily organs.

Philo, a Jewish mystic who lived in Egypt from 15 BCE to 50 CE, was the first to apply an allegorical reading to the Torah. In Philo's reading of *Exodus*, which recounts Moses leading the Israelites out of Egypt and back to the promised land, Egypt is allegorically considered to represent a body-dominated state of awareness, while Egypt's Pharaoh symbolises the lower, sense-occupied self. Moses is the perfect man, while the promised land is the state of possessing spiritual knowledge. The waters of the Red Sea that were held back so Moses and his people could cross, Philo interpreted as the practice of controlling the passions. The exodus itself represents a psychospiritual journey from a sense-focused existence to a spiritual one. While Philo's approach relied on extracting meanings not intended by the original writers, he pioneered the way of reading mystic depths into orthodox texts.

The first century Talmudic rabbis adopted Philo's allegorical reading, using the Sefirot to reveal hidden depths in *The Song of Songs*. The Sefirot comprises the ten attributes that Ein Sof (The Infinite) used to create the cosmos. These ten attributes are also present within each human being. The Talmudic mystics emphasised the unified action of the male aspect, Yesod, which included the phallus, with Malkut-Kingship, the female aspect, also known as the entrance and the receptacle.

During the thirteenth century, Spanish Jews extended this allegorical reading, incorporating it into the Kabbalah. Their Kabbalistic reading of *The Song Of Songs* similarly interpreted the female as Malkhut-Kingship, and the male as either incorporating all the attributes of Zer Anpin, or just Yesod. In this way the poem's eroticism was interpreted as mystic entrancement. One of the founders of modern Kabbalah, Rabbi Isaac Luria, used this interpretation of the *Songs*' imagery when creating his *Hymn for the Sabbath Eve*:

> I sing in hymns to enter the gates
> of the Field of holy apples.
> A new table we prepare for Her,
> a lovely candelabrum sheds its light on us.
> Between right and left the Bride approaches,
> in holy jewels and festive garments.
> Her Husband embraces Her in Her foundation,
> giving Her pleasure, squeezing out his strength.

> She has seventy crowns and the supernal King,
> that all may be crowned in the Holy of Holies.
> May it be His will that He dwell among His people,
> who take joy for His sake with sweets and honey.³

Rabbi Luria's poem introduces another aspect of the mystical perspective. Malkhut-Kingdom is also associated with Shekhinah, the Divine Presence, which is defined as "He who dwells among His people". It is through Shekhinah that Ein Sof is considered to fill the world with Presence and so to be immanent in all that is. Hence when a spiritual seeker wishes to experience Ein Sof, the entrance is via Malkhut-Kingdom. Through the practice of meditation and prayer, the seeker becomes the Bride preparing for her Divine husband's embrace.

This same concept was also explored by Christian mystics in their doctrine of spiritual marriage.

CHRISTIANITY'S MYSTIC MARRIAGE

Like many rabbis, orthodox Christian exegetes shied from an erotic interpretation of *The Song of Songs*, interpreting lover and beloved as worshipper and Church. This was interiorised by mystics like St John of the Cross, who read lover and beloved as seeker and Christ. This led to the creation of his remarkable tribute to the *Songs*, *Spiritual Canticle*, which begins:

> Where have you hidden, my love,
> leaving me distraught and alone?
> You wounded me
> then fled like a deer:
> I chased you, crying, but you were gone.⁴

St John of the Cross began composing his poem in 1577, after his spiritual superiors imprisoned him in a tiny cell, from which he was allowed out only for a weekly public lashing. St John used the nine months of imprisonment to compose *Spiritual Canticle* in his head, writing it down only after he had escaped. Years later a group of Carmelite nuns, to whom he had become confessor, asked him to write a commentary on his poem, as they found the poem's inner meaning difficult to penetrate. St John obliged, centering his interpretation on the concept of the mystic marriage between bride and bridegroom, who represented a seeker's soul and Christ. It is a developmental relationship, because before mystic marriage can take place, the bride has to prepare herself. First is the purgative stage, which involves physical and psychological purification. Next is the illuminative stage, in which the soul begins to receive spiritual insights. Finally comes marriage itself, in which the soul unites with Christ.

One of the influences on the Christian concept of spiritual marriage was Hermetic alchemy, which aimed to achieve a chemical wedding between the Red King and White Queen. This was intended allegorically, with the King and Queen working on several levels, simultaneously symbolising red sulphur and mercury, male and female energies, spirit and matter, and sun and moon. This notion of a chemical wedding was subsequently reworked by Christian mystics into the teaching that the mystic's soul is a bride who "marries" the Divine Presence.[5]

In *The Adornment of the Spiritual Marriage*, an influential late medieval Christian mystic text, Jan de Ruysbroeck described what preparation for mystic marriage entailed. Like St John of the Cross, he divided the process into three stages, which he termed active, interior and superessential. The active stage involves expunging the soul of negative habits and traits, and striving to live morally. This coincides with St John's purgative stage. The goal of this stage is for the potential bride to make herself pleasing so Christ, the Bridegroom, will accept her.

Next the bride shifts her attention from things and creatures of the world and focuses on her interior life. This is where the encounter with Christ will occur. Regarding the significance of this stage, St John (using the essence-presence dichotomy created by his fellow Spanish Kabbalah mystics) stated: "We must remember that the Word, the Son of God, together with the Father and the Holy Spirit, is hidden in essence and in presence, in the inmost being of the soul. That soul, therefore, that will find Him, must go out from all things in will and affection, and enter into the profoundest self-recollection, and all things must be to it as if they existed not. ... God is therefore hidden within the soul, and the true contemplative will seek Him there in love, saying, "Where have You hidden Yourself?"[6]

During Ruysbroeck's interior stage the seeking bride undertakes spiritual exercises to purify the will, intellect and emotions, and to practise the inner virtues of patience, humility, discernment, and obedience. These exercises enable the spirit to be filled with the light of Spirit and suffused with love. The model here is Christ himself, who embodies all the inner qualities that the soul as bride needs in preparation for the arrival of Christ.

The third stage Ruysbroeck termed superessential. He called this stage the God-seeing life. St John of the Cross called this stage the unitive way of spiritual marriage. Here Christ enters the soul via a place hidden deep within. In Ruysbroek's words: "The eyes with which the spirit contemplates and gazes upon its Bridegroom are so widely dilated that they will never again be closed. For the gazing and contemplation of the spirit remain eternally fixed on the hidden revelation of God."[7]

The spirit now reaches the beatific state that St John described in the final stanzas of his *Spiritual Canticle*:

> Let us rejoice, my Beloved! ...
> We shall go at once
> to the deep caverns in the rock,
> into secret places,
> hidden from sight,
> where we shall drink ancient wine ...
> The breathing of the air,
> the song of the sweet nightingale,
> the grove and its beauty
> in the serene night,
> with the flame that consumes and gives no pains.[8]

St John allegorically interprets the *deep caverns in the rock* as the inward place where the mysteries, attributes and power of Presence are revealed. Hence it is one of the *secret places, hidden from sight*. Elucidating the last five lines, St John wrote: "The soul refers here, under five different expressions, to that which the Bridegroom is to give it in the beatific transformation. 1. The aspiration of the Holy Spirit of God after it, and its own aspiration after God. 2. Joyous praise of God in the fruition of Him. 3. The knowledge of creatures and the order of them. 4. The pure and clear contemplation of the divine essence. 5. Perfect transformation in the infinite love of God."[9]

THIS COLLECTION'S OTHER SOURCES

The second primary source for the poems presented here is, clearly, the *Psalms*. For the Talmudic mystics, the *Psalms* were not only profound texts that describe a wide variety of spiritual states, they were sung to induce elevated states. As Aryeh Kaplan explains: "In the Talmudic tradition there is a clear indication that the Psalms were used to attain the state of enlightenment called Ruach HaKodesh. If one looks at many psalms, one sees that they begin with either the phrase, 'A Psalm of David' or 'Of David, a Psalm.' The Talmud states that when a psalm begins with the phrase, 'Of David, a Psalm,' this indicates that he recited the psalm after he had attained Ruach HaKodesh. But when a psalm begins with 'A Psalm of David,' it means that David actually made use of the psalm in order to attain his state of enlightenment. Thus at least eighteen psalms were specifically composed as a means of attaining higher states of consciousness."[10]

Scholars today consider David wrote possibly half the *Psalms*. Of the remainder, seven writers have been identified, including Solomon, who wrote two, and Moses, to whom one is ascribed. These are conjectural assignations. The rest have unknown authors. The collection was likely written over a period of several hundred years, from the time when the first Jerusalem Temple was still in use, with the earliest psalms being sung during worship. The last psalms date to post-Exilic times, with the collection as a whole likely having been edited by around 200 BCE. While there are several theories regarding the organisation of the *Psalms*, no overarching structure has been agreed. However, groupings may be discerned, with psalms falling into the broad categories of hymn, lament, acknowledgement of royalty, expressions of individual pain and thanksgiving.

My own response to the *Psalms* has been to draw on them to illustrate aspects of the soul's spiritual journey from disassociation to unity. In organising them in this way, I have been inspired by Farid ud-Din Attar's thirteenth century Sufi poem, *Conference of the Birds*. This is an allegorical poem which describes the journey undertaken by a group of thirty birds on a quest to find the mysterious Simurgh. Their journey involves crossing seven valleys, each representing a stage in the spiritual quest. Each bird also represents a particular human psychological failing. In the Persian language, in which Attar wrote, *si* means thirty and *murgh* means bird. So when the birds eventually find the Simurgh, in effect they find themselves. For my psalms I have created a hybrid, adopting Farid ud-Din Attar's structure of a journey, but moving it through the three phases identified by Christian mystics rather than seven valleys, and replacing the thirty birds on pilgrimage with Judaic mysticism's seeker (human essence) who unites with his beloved (spiritual presence). Attar's journey, which culminates in the birds' reaching the Simurgh, is also the journey back to Jerusalem, our spiritual home.

The third Judaic influence is the poetry of *Isaiah*. Due to the powerful way *Isaiah* addresses invasion, defeat, exile, judgement and redemption, it became the most popular prophetic book among post-Exilic Jews. Its evocations of a coming messiah, which Christian exegetes interpreted as Jesus Christ, made it just as revered by later Christian readers. *Isaiah* consequently became the prophetic book most quoted in New Testament writings. Through the St James translation, *Isaiah* has had a significant impact on the English language, contributing several well-known phrases, such as new heaven and new earth, man of sorrows, drop in the bucket and like a lamb to the slaughter.

Scholars consider *Isaiah* had at least three writers. Chapters 1 to 39 were written by the prophet Isaiah ben Amoz, who lived in the eighth century BCE. An anonymous author wrote chapters 40 to 55 several decades later, during the Exile. After the exiles had returned to Judah, several unknown authors added chapters 56 to 66. This last era, which began in 516 BCE, is known as the Second Temple period, as it was at this time that a new temple was built on Temple Mount in Jerusalem, to replace the original temple destroyed by Nebuchadnezzar eighty years earlier. The Second Temple stood until 70 CE, when it was destroyed by the Romans in response to a Jewish uprising.

Isaiah is not an explicitly mystic work, although passages were read as mystical by the Second Temple rabbis. One key section is Chapter Six, in which Isaiah describes his vision of Yahweh in a heavenly temple. This vision became foundational to temple mysticism. It was also linked to Ezekiel's vision in which he was taken up to heaven in a chariot, a vision that became foundational to Merkabah (chariot) mysticism. Among much striking poetry, the second Isaiah writer also produced the first clear statement of the monotheism adopted by the Abrahamic religions: "I am the first and I am the last; besides me there is no God." (*Isaiah* 44:6).

The final work that has contributed to my approach here is by the Sufi master, Muhyiddin Ibn 'Arabi. Called Shaykh al-Akbar (the Greatest Shaykh) due to the breadth and depth of his knowledge, *Tarjumán al-Ashwáq (The Interpreter of Desire),* is his poetic masterwork. Written in Arabic, it is a sequence of love poems in which Ibn 'Arabi celebrated a Meccan sheik's beautiful daughter. Pilgrimage is a central theme, with both the annual Muslim hajj and life on the pilgrimage trail featuring prominently. After critics accused Ibn 'Arabi of writing erotic poems, he added a commentary, in which he used an allegorical reading to reveal how his poems' apparently profane surfaces hid profound mystic depths. Both the metaphor of spirituality as a pilgrimage, and Ibn 'Arabi's allegorical readings of his own poems, contributed to my conceiving of the journey depicted in these psalms.

It is fitting that the mystic traditions of Judaism, Christianity, and Islam have influenced this collection, for these traditions also share two ideas that are directly relevant to the mystic perspective: that spiritual experiences are available to all who seek them, and that a transcendent Presence, however conceived and named, is at the heart of such experiences.

OUR DIFFICULTY WITH THE ANCIENT MYSTICS

The sources I have been referencing constitute a highly technical literature, which is not easily digested by us today. Indeed, despite the mystics quoted so far drawing on their own distinct Judaic, Christian or Islamic heritages, they had more in common with each other than with us today, given our outlook is dominated by materialism. Despite their cultural differences, the mystics of Judaism, Christianity and Islam drew on a shared world view, philosophic vocabulary, and allegorical method, so when St John referred to the Divine Presence, and used phrases such as *hiding away from all creatures* and *seeking the secret chamber*, his meaning was readily understood by educated European and Middle Eastern readers from the second century BCE to 1700 CE. However, such language is far from accessible today, becoming meaningful only after considerable study and exegesis.

Nonetheless, one crucial aspect unites us with those mystics. That is our ability to experience Presence for ourselves. In *Omens of the Millennium,* American literary critic Harold Bloom noted a late twentieth century shift towards experiential spirituality. He observed that over the millennia Western religions had come to emphasise the institutional, historical and dogmatic, in which Deity was assumed to exist outside the self. But mystics and visionaries within those religious traditions had always advocated "an alternative convention, the way of Gnosis, [involving] an acquaintance with, or knowledge of, the

God within."[11] According to Bloom, during the late twentieth century people's religious engagement has reflected the mystic approach, shifting from institutional conformity to a freer form of gnosis.

Gnosis, in its most general sense, without linking it to the historical movement of Gnosticism, is knowledge derived from direct experience. In Sufism, gnosis is called *ma'arif*; in Judaism, chariot and throne mysticism are grounded in gnostic experience of Presence. The trend Bloom identified, of people shifting from being primarily institutionally and doctrinally focused to being more concerned with their own direct, personal spiritual experience, is now widespread. It is popularly characterised as being "spiritual but not religious". Those who identify themselves in this way tend to participate in the grassroots meditation, prayer, yoga, metaphysical and self-transformational groups that have proliferated around the world. This experiential, gnostic approach also conceives of Deity differently. Where institutionalised religions see God as transcendent and distant, and others accordingly conceive of Deity as detached, even indifferent, those who practise spirituality as gnostic encounter consider Deity to be immanent, close, engaged. Such a Deity is not a being, but Being itself.

This widespread trend aligns with the mystic intent. However, historically mystics taught that integrating our individual awareness with Presence requires sustained focus, effort and energy. To do so we first have to recognise and purify our psychospiritual self. Only then are we in a position to open up our everyday awareness to Presence.

All this is a prelude to what follows, in which I offer a brief mystic interpretation of the forty psalms presented here. My comments are intended to explicate the psalms' imagery, ideas and terminology, as adapted from the work of the Hebrew prophets. I then use texts drawn from the mystic traditions of Judaism, Christianity and Islam to clarify the imagery's mystic intent. My aim is to indicate the phases of spiritual growth from spiritual dissociation to unity that the sequence embodies, while using the allegorical method of interpretation our forebears pioneered to interpret the sequence.

IN BABYLON

The first section explores the spiritual seeker's point of departure. The world that must be left behind is called Babylon. For the Hebrew prophets, Babylon represented the non-spiritual. As the prophet Jeremiah wrote: "In Babylon you will see gods made of silver, of gold, of wood, being carried shoulder high ... Plated with gold and silver, their tongues polished smooth by a craftsman, they are counterfeit and have no power to speak."[12] Using today's vocabulary, Babylon symbolises the inner state of being caught up in wholly materialistic experience. For exiled Judaeans, the place they wished to escape to was their home of Jerusalem. So where Babylon symbolises entrapment in the material physical world, Jerusalem symbolises the immaterial spiritual realm.

Baal was one of Babylon's principal gods, and so became a target for the Jewish prophets. In the poems, Baal represents the distractions that divert human attention away from its inner spiritual nature and towards material existence. *Each day Babylon's soldiers guard mute / gods made of gold. Their words, pronounced / by priests, enthral empty souls.* Supporting Baal are soldiers, representing sense perceptions, and temple priests, who provide the justifications for a purely material existence. But the priests are not entirely external. From a psychospiritual perspective, the priests are those aspects of our personality that cause us to view reality as exclusively physical and to doubt or deny our own spiritual dimension.

Nebuchadnezzar is the king who rules Babylon. He represents the ego that rules our inner life. Sufis call the ego the commanding self, because it is an imperious king, demanding we spend all our time, energy and efforts on it. In relation to this, St John observed: "The soul feels itself as if it were in the land of enemies, tyrannised over by the stranger, like the dead among the dead. ... This misery of the soul, in the captivity of the body, is thus spoken of by Jeremiah: 'Is Israel a bondman or a home-born slave? Why then is he become a prey? The lions have roared upon him, and have made a noise.' The lions are the desires and the rebellious motions of the tyrant king of sensuality."[13]

In order to set out on a journey towards their own deep reality, seekers need to shift their attention from being wholly immersed in what is happening in the world and to pay more attention to their inner world. Such a movement of attention is symbolised in the poems by *dawn* and *dusk*. Dawn signifies a state of engagement with the material world, while dusk is a state of disconnecting from the external and directing attention within. When seekers enter themselves, St John considered they enter a darkness in which they "set out upon the road and way of the spirit, which is ... called the way of illumination or of infused contemplation, wherein God Himself feeds and refreshes the soul. Such, as we have said, is the night and purgation of sense in the soul."[14]

The body is popularly called the temple of God. The mystic view is that the temple consists of our whole being. The body is the exterior and visible part of our being, but many other aspects of us exist within the temple. There are the porticos, the five senses, while the public galleries represent our motor, instinctive, emotional, and intellectual facilities, which we use to process sense impressions and to interact with people and situations in the world external to us. Deeper within is the altar on which we place the energy generated by our daily actions. This altar is supported by our attitudes and motives, some of which we are consciously aware, others we don't perceive or understand. Deeper still is the chamber of the heart, which is hidden until we look within. Then there are those profoundly secret places of which we only become aware after extensive exploration. Chief among these places is the seat of our own consciousness, the spiritual self, also called the soul.

The soul is described in the poems as a virgin. Meister Eckhart defines a virgin as "a person who is free of irrelevant ideas, as free as he was before he was born."[15] Our spiritual soul existed before we were born. It transcends all our actions and life circumstances, as well as our own assumptions of what presence and spirituality might be. Our soul can be imprisoned inside us, covered up, hidden, but it remains always itself, transcendent and pure.

The temple of our being in its fallen and undeveloped state exists in Babylon, but in its risen and developed state it takes its place in Jerusalem. In Jerusalem is Mount Zion. Mystically, Mount Zion symbolizes silence. It is in silence that mystic revelation becomes manifest. Psychospiritually, the journey from Babylon to Jerusalem is inward. We don't abandon our body, we don't die; instead, the journey consists of a shift in the focus and expansiveness of our awareness.

Rare individuals easily connect with the inner spiritual realm. The rest of us require guidance to get us there. Several forms of guidance are referred to in the poems. The first is via dreams. Abraham comes to the seeker in a dream. The seeker also dreams of his lost lover. In these dreams he receives knowledge that aids his search. The second form of guidance consists of visions, which are experienced while awake. They also provide insights. The third is oral instruction from a teacher who has mastered an area of knowledge or expertise. Books can also function as teachers, being generally less flexible variations on oral teaching. The fourth form of guidance consists of subtle signs observed in the midst of daily life. These reveal aspects of Presence's activity in the world. Collectively, guidance and signs open up the path seekers need to follow in order to learn, grow and progress.

From the mystic perspective, the world is Presence's activity. When we start out on the spiritual quest, we do not appreciate this. But when we are able to directly discern Presence's activity in the world, the world becomes transformed—not because the world has changed, but because our perspective has changed. Thus, when we are in an unreceptive state the world will divert us, but when we are in a receptive state it instructs us. As Ibn 'Arabi wrote: "The only reason God multiplied the signs in the world and in ourselves—for we are part of the world—was so that we might turn our gaze toward it with remembrance, reflection, intelligence, faith, knowledge, hearing, sight, understanding, and mind."[16]

The purpose of guidance is to help us develop our inner faculties so we may eventually perceive directly, without intermediaries. To achieve this seekers need to develop their capacity to experience higher states. Adopting qualities such as tenacity, self-belief, faith, love, and discernment help to develop this capacity. In the poems, *babies, children, sons* and *daughters* represent these qualities.

Mystically, the slave's beloved has been interpreted in different ways. For St John the beloved is Christ, the Bridegroom, which the soul seeks to embrace: "That the thirsty soul may find the Bridegroom, and be one with Him in the union of love in this life—so far as that is possible ... we must remember that the Word, the Son of God, together with the Father and the Holy Spirit, is hidden in essence and in presence, in the inmost being of the soul. That soul, therefore, that will find Him, must go out from all things in will and affection, and enter into the profoundest self-recollection, and all things must be to it as if they existed not."[17] St John refers here to essence and presence. Essence consists of the active aspect, which is termed male, while presence consists of the female aspect, which experiences and absorbs spiritual influences when we are in a passive inner state. For Jewish mystics, the relationship between lover and beloved is between between the active inner male and passive female parts. Of this relationship, Aryeh Kaplan wrote:

> Zer Anpin is what is usually referred to as the 'Supernal Man', and it is with regard to Zer Anpin that it is written that 'God made Man is His image' (*Genesis* 1:27). In the spiritual realm, when two things resemble each other, they are said to be in proximity, and one can be a vehicle for the other. Therefore, since Man is a counterpart of Zer Anpin, it is through Zer Anpin that Man can become a vehicle for the supernal. Man then binds himself to the Female, just as the male cleaves to the female in a physical sense. The Female is the Divine Presence. ... Earning reward is through Zer Anpin, while receiving reward is through the Female. Zer Anpin therefore consists of the six Sefirot (which include strength, love, and beauty) and corresponds to the six working days, while the Female corresponds to the Sabbath.[18]

Spiritually, men and women equally possess active essence and passive presence. Receiving via passive presence is achieved only by temporarily stopping active essence's engagement with the world, then entering a heightened state of awareness. Such a state is alluded to in the poems by the words *dusk, night, darkness, moon,* and *bed.*

How is this heightened state achieved? Prayer and meditation are used worldwide. That the ancient Hebrew prophets used prayer to communicate with the spiritual realm is obvious. Their use of meditation is less known. Aryeh Kaplan has shown that the prophets used meditation to induce dreams, visions and altered states of awareness: "The prophets would meditate on the highest mysteries of the Sefirot, as well as on the Supernal Soul. ... When their soul became attached to the Supernal Soul, this vision would be increased and intensified. It would then be revealed automatically through a state where thought is utterly absent. ... It was in this manner that the earthly saints raised their thoughts, reaching the place from which their souls emanated."[19]

With mind clear, heart focused, and an understanding of the path to be travelled, the seeker is now ready to escape from the prison that is Babylon and begin the journey to humanity's spiritual home of Jerusalem.

IN THE WILDERNESS

In Babylon the seeker is a slave, in the sense that awareness is limited to bodily existence and so is enslaved by it. In this next phase the seeker enters the wilderness of the self. The self is a wilderness because it is yet devoid of knowledge, lacks inner unity, and possesses no deep understanding. The seeker's task is to become a shepherd, gathering the scattered inner parts and resources, then getting them to function harmoniously. This is how the seeker begins to grow psychospiritually.

Inner growth involves two tasks. The first is to develop

innate qualities, skills and talents. The second is to reduce and eventually eliminate the negative attitudes and emotions that stop us from utilising our innate qualities skills and talents and developing them to their potential. Negative attitudes that are self-limiting include scepticism, self-justification, arrogance and lack of trust. Examples of negative emotions are jealousy, fear, greed and self-pity. In the poems, the *five soldiers* represent the five senses, while *the desert people* who buffet and steal from the shepherd symbolise negativities. Conversely, *the three dogs* the shepherd has to train represent his motor, emotional and intellectual parts, with the *staff* representing discerning practices that stimulate growth. Growing our inner parts, and eliminating limiting factors from our psychology, provides us with the capacity, strength and energy to sustain the journey. Three tests then present themselves.

The first test is when the new shepherd realizes how difficult this task is. The *goats*, *sheep* and *dogs* represent a triad of inner aspects that have to be awakened, kept in check, and developed. For medieval Christian theologians, the soul possessed a tripartite make-up that consisted of understanding, will and memory:"The soul speaks of three things that distress it: namely, languor, suffering, and death. ... In the understanding, it languishes because it does not see God, Who is the salvation of it. ... In the will, it suffers because it does not possess God, Who is its comfort and delight. ... In the memory, it dies because it remembers its lack of all the blessings of the understanding, which are the vision of God, and of the delights of the will, which are the fruition of Him."[20]

Today we could characterise the *goats*, *sheep* and *dogs* on different levels: physically, as consisting of movement, emotions and thought; psychologically, as traits that promote focus, distraction and sound navigation through the world; and spiritually, as opening up (to Presence), surrendering (in order to absorb what arrives), and manifesting (what is absorbed). Yet, however we characterise our inner parts, the task of shepherding them involves overcoming, in St John's words, "the languor, suffering, and death" that assail us on all levels of our being. Marshalling our resources and overcoming whatever inwardly makes our progress difficult, or that even strives to kill it off, is challenging work.

The second test is dealing with inner aridity. Aridity is a common experience for spiritual seekers, who long to be filled with Presence but just experience emptiness. Aridity arises due to our tastes changing: material processes and experiences that previously attracted us no longer do, but we have not yet gathered sufficient immaterial resources to create an inner life to replace them. St John wrote: "The cause of this aridity is that God transfers to the spirit the good things and the strength of the senses ... If it [the soul] is not immediately conscious of spiritual sweetness and delight, but only of aridity and lack of sweetness, the reason for this is the strangeness of the exchange; for its palate has been accustomed to those other sensual pleasures upon which its eyes are still fixed."[21]

Underlying these first two tests is the process of inner death. One of the hadiths (traditional sayings) of the Holy Prophet, Muhammad, is that we must die before we die. This is also the process referred to in the death and resurrection of Lazarus as related in *John's Gospel*: we first must die to be reborn. Eliminating negative emotions, and changing limiting attitudes and false ideas, involves a series of inner deaths. It is only by eliminating what holds us back that we can continue on our journey. A by-product of these inner deaths is that a lesser resurrection follows each, for resurrection, like all else on the spiritual journey, occurs progressively, and on a number of levels. One death leads to a birth, the fruits of which in turn fall away, resulting in our entering a new, higher phase. And so on.

The third test hinges on our response when inner aridity is replaced by gifts, growth and spiritual experiences. It is illustrated in the poem that describes the shepherd arriving at a wadi. This test arises after seekers begin to reap the results of spiritual growth, which is experienced in the form of gifts that manifest as insights and increased abilities. Gifts can be just as destabilising as aridity, for where continued dryness results in seekers becoming downhearted, gifts can so profoundly shake the seekers' sense of self and reality that progress is halted while what happened they struggle to integrate what happened into their awareness. Then the test becomes one of discerning between what is useful and so warrants further exploration, and what is interesting but ultimately not to be pursued. On the other hand, what arrives may be so different from what the seeker expected that it takes time (perhaps a long time) to process it and decide whether to accept it at face value, reject it, repackage it conceptually into something more recognisable and comfortable, or use it to completely realign one's outlook and approach.

In relation to this, Sufis distinguish between states, which are temporary experiences, and stations, which signify permanent levels of spiritual development. The Sufi teacher, Hujwiri, described the difference in this way:

> Station denotes anyone's standing in the Way of God, and one's fulfilment of the obligations appertaining to that station, and one's keeping it until one comprehends its perfection so far as lies in humanity's power. It is not permissible that one should quit one's station without fulfilling the obligations thereof. Thus, the

first station is repentance, then comes conversion, then renunciation, then trust in God, and so on. ... State, on the other hand, is something that descends from God into one's heart, without one being able to repel it when it comes, or attract it when it goes, by personal effort. ... Station belongs to the category of acts, state to the category of gifts.[22]

What is significant in relation to states is how we respond to their gifts. Do we stop to enjoy them, get lost in them and as a consequence forget our quest? Or do we sip briefly, enjoy the moment, absorb the lessons, then continue on our way?

Spiritual gifts are experienced at a deep level, enabling seekers to experience their own deep selves. This is explored in the poems that describe the shepherd meeting his beloved: *That night, in my tent, my existence / was transformed: from the darkness stepped / she for whom I was born*. Night symbolises the state of inner disengagement from sense perceptions, it facilitates a new order of experiences and knowledge.

Conversely, sometimes we are gifted a severe storm or trial. Regarding them, St John observed: "As a rule, these storms and trials are sent [to seekers] by God ... to the end that, when they have been chastened and buffeted, they may through them prepare themselves. ... For if the soul is not tempted, exercised, and proved with trials and temptations, it cannot appreciate Wisdom."[23]

In other words, having to overcome adversity requires us to draw on our personal resources, which strengthens us inwardly, so we become better equipped to cope with what comes next. Which is Wisdom.

The earliest Jewish Wisdom literature consisted of homilies: "On the lips of the discerning man is wisdom found, on the back of a fool, the stick."[24] Here Wisdom is a general term, associated with moral good. Later generations personified Wisdom into the embodiment of moral good: "On the hilltop, on the road, at the crossroads, she takes her stand ... 'O men, I am calling to you. ... I, Wisdom, am mistress of discretion, the inventor of lucidity of thought. Good advice and sound judgment belong to me. ... I walk in the way of virtue, in the paths of justice, enriching those who love me, filling their treasuries'."[25] Later again, influenced by Greek philosophy, a metaphysical level was added to Wisdom: "Yahweh created me when his purpose first unfolded, before the oldest of his works. From everlasting I was firmly set, from the beginning, before the Earth came into being. ... I was by his side, a master craftsman, delighting him day after day, ever at play in his presence, at play everywhere in the world, delighting to be with the sons of men."[26]

Jewish mystics developed this metaphysical concept of Wisdom even further in the model of the Sefirot: "In order for a totally transcendental God to relate to His creation, a series of Ten Sefirot [emanations] had to be brought into existence. The first two of these Sefirot are Keter-Crown and Chakhmah-Wisdom. The first Sefirot is called the Crown, since a crown is worn above the head. The Crown therefore refers to things that are above the mind's abilities of comprehension. Wisdom is therefore the first thing that the mind can grasp. ... Wisdom is the conduit of the Creator's Essence, and it therefore sustains all things. As the link between Creator and creation, it is the vehicle for the potential of all things. The Talmud thus says, 'Who has Wisdom? He who sees the unborn.'"[27] The unborn is the spiritual self.

Ibn 'Arabi offers another perspective on this same idea: "God is Being, while the things are the forms of Being. So the entire affair is interconnected. ... There cannot be existence except from two roots: one root is power, which is linked to the side of God; the second root is reception, which is linked to the side of the possible thing. ... For God is the Wise, and in each thing He has a manifest wisdom. The People of Unveiling and Finding know what that wisdom is in all things."[28]

For St John, Wisdom is associated with the Presence that Christianity calls Christ: "The soul that will go out of the house of its own will, abandoning the bed of its own satisfaction, will find the divine Wisdom, the Son of God, the Bridegroom waiting at the door."[29]

Wisdom grows as seekers connect with their own spiritual self. Wisdom, like other forms of knowledge, is not easily won. Deep knowledge is subtle, and seekers often become confused as to whether what they think they are receiving is valid. Confusion results from not being sure where subtle impulses are coming from, and whether they are valuable, misleading, imagined, or are being misinterpreted. This last is a common issue, because all seekers have ideas and attitudes they were taught when young, or adopted of their own volition down the years. These received ideas and attitudes may be valid, partially valid, invalid, irrelevant, wrong or misleading. It takes years to learn how to interpret one's own deep experiences. This is all part of developing wisdom.

Wisdom gained manifests in continuing deep perceptions and experiences, in an ability to perceive others' situations at a deep level, and in an ability to appreciate spiritual texts, becoming able to reinterpret them and recontextualise them so they may usefully cast light on current situations and dilemmas for the benefit on oneself and others.

IN JERUSALEM

Finally, the seeker (essence) and his beloved (presence) arrive in Jerusalem. They find a garden full of flowers, fruit, vines, and pomegranates, where little foxes dart and wine flows from Wisdom's cup. St John wrote: "This garden is the soul itself ... because the flowers of perfection and the virtues planted in it flourish and grow."[30]

Entering this inner garden indicates seekers have developed and reintegrated their inner parts to a level in which the role of shepherd has been outgrown. They now become a servant.

Seekers struggle for years through the wilderness, battling with doubt, aridity, temptations and gifts, learning step by step to shepherd their inner resources. In the process, they develop their abilities, talents and strength. But in order to live in Jerusalem, seekers then have to place all they have developed at the service of their inner self, and perform whatever tasks they have been alloted. This process is referred to symbolically in the imagery of the *lion* and *lamb* sharing the hills: the lion of action (male, human essence) has to lie down and allow the lambs of passivity (female, spiritual presence) to gambol and play. It is also symbolised by the seeker no longer leading the beloved, but instead following her lead: *Her kiss / suffuses my heart, and gently she lifts me / into the sky's glowing arch.*

This new inner relationship of mystic servanthood is explored in the symbolism of sacred marriage. As a symbol, the sacred marriage dates back to the Neolithic era, when the Earth Goddess, whose fertility caused crops to grow, was ritually married to the tribe's most potent male at midwinter, in order to usher in spring. By the Bronze Age, the sacred marriage had been anthropomorphized into male-female pairings such as the Egyptian Isis and Osiris, the Sumerian Ishtar and Tammuz, and the Greek Zeus and Hera. During the Iron Age city-states developed, populations became increasingly urbanized, and nature's direct impact on people's lives started to diminish. New modes of expression, reflecting their lifestyles, became widely disseminated. Study of the movements of the stars led to the development of astrology, which was originally designed to help seekers understand the constituent parts of their inner make-up. Metallurgy, which blended metals into new alloys, inspired the development of inner alchemy. This used the symbolism of lead being transmuted into gold to teach seekers how to transform their own psychospiritual self.

As noted earlier, because humanity's cultural context has changed so radically, these teachings have lost much of their relevance, even if astrology still intrigues many. Yet the psychospiritual practices behind astrology and inner alchemy continue to be relevant. This is especially the case in cultures where the female principle has low status in relation to the male. In mystical traditions that promote the discipline of sacred marriage, not only are the male and female principles seen as equal, it is considered spiritually necessary for the active male aspects of the self to become passive to, and to follow the lead of, the psyche's female aspects.

This is the background for the sacred marriage providing a potent symbol for spiritual rejuvenation and integration. Richard of St Victor, a late medieval Christian mystic, divided the sacred marriage into four phases. "The first phase is betrothal, in which the soul commits to the Beloved and purifies itself in preparation for the second phase, which is marriage. Marriage involves the act of inner contemplation, in which the soul rises above itself, experiencing the higher spiritual realities symbolised by the Beloved. In this phase the soul sees the Beloved, but remains separate from Him. The third phase is wedlock, in which the soul and the Beloved are united, and the soul is transformed into something new. The fourth phase is fruitfulness, in which the soul returns to the world and uses what it has experienced to help others who are undertaking the same journey."[31]

The Kabbalah represents this same mystic development through the symbol of the throne. Throne symbolism is derived from the vision of the prophet Ezekiel, when he saw four strange creatures accompanied by four wheels. Above the creatures he saw a firmament, and "above the firmament that was over their heads was the likeness of a throne ... and on the likeness of the throne was the likeness of the appearance of a Man upon it from above."[32]

The Kabbalists teach that Ezekiel saw four universes: Atzilut (Closeness), Beriyah (Creation), Yetzirah (Formation), and Asiyah (Making). Atzilut, the highest, is the realm of the Ten Sefirot, the emanations of the Infinite, which is represented in Ezekiel's vision by the Man on the throne. Beriyah is the creative realm, symbolized by the throne. The Infinite "lowers" Itself into the throne, which is a poetic way of saying that on this level the creative forces which emanate from the Infinite are arrayed in preparation for manifestation into the lower levels. "The part of the human soul that reaches the level of Beriyah is that of the Neshamah. This highest level of the soul is the 'breath of God', and represents the first stage of God's 'lowering' Himself to create man and be concerned with his destiny."[33] The third level is Yetzirah. This is the realm of the angels, these being the forces that connect the Infinite with the fourth level, Asiyah. Asiyah is the realm of making, which consists of the physical world and includes those spiritualised aspects which interact with it and with the levels above.

Ibn 'Arabi also identified four worlds. For him, the highest is subsistence, the spiritual realm. Next is the world of transmutation, constituted of the elements of ether, fire, air, water, earth, themselves existing in seven strata. Third is the world of habitation, which includes the spiritual, animal, vegetative and mineral. Fourth is the world of relations, variously consisting of psychological factors, accident, quantity, position and so on. Of the highest world, he wrote: "That is the Muhammadan Reality, whose sphere is Life. Its equivalent in man is the subtle reality, the holy spirit. Included within this world is the All-Encompassing throne, whose equivalent in man is the body. Of this world is the Footstool, whose equivalent in man is the soul. Of it is the Inhabited House, whose equivalent in man is the heart. Of it are the angels, whose equivalents in man are the spirits and faculties within him."[34]

For Ibn 'Arabi, as for his fellow Jewish and Christian mystics, the seeker's quest for integration involves an ascent through a series of inner levels that are characterised as stations and worlds. While the concepts and vocabularies differ, the Jewish, Christian and Islamic mystical traditions all describe a similar process in which seekers progress through the many levels within their own being in order to eventually integrate their everyday awareness with their expansive self and, through it, experience what exists in the Beyond.

Such progress culminates in servanthood. Of this Ibn 'Arabi commented: "The station of servanthood is the station of lowliness and poverty."[35] Lowliness refers to removing self-focus from our motives and attitude when carrying out activities. Poverty refers to surrendering all that adheres to our being, including abilities we develop through our own efforts, gifts that arrive through grace, and experiences we have along the way. The ultimate goal is to embrace the mystery in the midst of which we live.

OUR TASK OF RE-INTEGRATION

While we are embodied, our task of integration is never complete, because we contain as yet undiscovered aspects of our self to explore and integrate into our everyday awareness. In addition, individual seekers have their own personal combinations of talents, abilities and gifts. Consequently, those we consider wise possess different varieties of knowledge, different levels of understanding, and use a variety of conceptual frameworks to express and share their wisdom. We reflect, on a lesser scale, the Infinite which manifests in more ways, and many more modalities, than we will ever comprehend.

I will end this introduction to the key concepts behind these psalms with the words of the great medieval Torah scholar and mystic, Moses Maimonides. He wrote of the spiritual journey:

> Individuals with the requisite qualities can delve into the mysteries, advancing in these deep, subtle concepts and gaining a firm understanding and perception of them. ... Such people must work on themselves until their mind is constantly clear and directed on high. They must bind their intellect to the Throne of Glory, striving to comprehend the purity and holiness of the transcendental. They must further contemplate on the wisdom of God in each thing, understanding its true significance, whether it be the highest spiritual entity or the lowliest thing on Earth. ... Individuals who do this ... become completely different people. They can now understand with a knowledge completely different to anything they have experienced before.[36]

REFERENCES

1. For a full consideration of the historical background to *The Song of Songs*, and for its best English language translation, see Chana and Ariel Bloch's *The Song of Songs*, New York: Modern Library, 2006.
2. Aryeh Kaplan, *The Bahir*, NY: Samuel Weiser, 1989, p 67.
3. Rabbi Isaac Luria, *Hymn for the Sabbath Eve*, in *Safed Spirituality: Rules of Mystical Piety, the Beginning of Wisdom*, translated by Lawrence Fine, New Jersey: Paulist Press, 1984, pp 78-79.
4. St John of the Cross, *A Spiritual Canticle of the Soul and the Bridegroom Christ*. This is the author's version of the first verse.
5. For a sketch of the chemical wedding see the author's *The New Mysticism*, Auckland: Attar Books, pp 67-69.
6. St John of the Cross, *A Spiritual Canticle of the Soul and the Bridegroom Christ*, translated by David Lewis, corrections and introduction by Benedict Zimmerman. Originally published in 1909, the text is now available online. The quotation is paragraph 7, from St John's exegesis of the poem's first line: *Where have You hidden Yourself?*
7. John of Ruysbroeck, *The Adornment of Spiritual Marriage, The Book of Truth, The Parkling Stone*, translated from the Flemish by C. A. Wynschenk DOM, edited with an introduction and notes by Evelyn Underhill, London: J.M. Dent & Sons, 1916. Originally written around 1350, Wynschenk's transla-

tion was most recently reprinted by Leopold Classic Library, 2016, but is also available online.

8   St John of the Cross, *A Spiritual Canticle*. Author's version of the poem's final stanzas.
9   St John of the Cross, *Dark Night of the Soul*, translated by E. Allison Peers, NY: Image Books, 1959, pp 40–41.
10 Aryeh Kaplan, *Meditation and the Bible*, NY: Samuel Weiser, 1988, pp 138–139.
11 Harold Bloom, *Omens of the Millennium: The Gnosis of Angels, Dreams, and Resurrection*, NY: Riverhead Books, 1996, p 1.
12 *The Jerusalem Bible*, Darton, Longman & Todd, London, 1966. Baruch 6:14–68.
13 St John of the Cross (Lewis), *A Spiritual Canticle*, p 75.
14 St John of the Cross (Peers), *Dark Night*, p 56.
15 Raymond Bernard Blakney, *Meister Eckhart*, NY: Harper & Row, 1941, p 207.
16 Ibn 'Arabi, *The Meccan Revelations, Vol 1*, edited by Michel Chodkiewicz, translations by William C. Chittick and James Morris, NY: Pir Press, 2002, p 182.
17 St John of the Cross (Lewis), *A Spiritual Canticle*, Stanza 1.6-7, p 13.
18 Kaplan, *The Bahir*, pp 131–132.
19 Kaplan, *Meditation and the Bible*, p 88.
20 St John of the Cross (Lewis), *A Spiritual Canticle*, p 21.
21 St John of the Cross (Peers), *Dark Night of the Soul*, pp 40–41.
22 Quoted by Sayyed Hossein Nasr, *Living Sufism*, Mandela Books, 1980, p 62.
23 St John of the Cross (Peers), *Dark Night of the Soul*, p 57.
24 *The Jerusalem Bible*, Proverbs 10:13.
25 Ibid, Proverbs 8:1–21.
26 Ibid, Proverbs 8:22–31.
27 *The Bahir*, pp 91–92.

28 *The Meccan Revelations*, pp 192–195.
29 St John of the Cross (Lewis), *A Spiritual Canticle*, p 24.
30 Ibid, p 72.
31 Evelyn Underhill, *Mysticism*, E.P. Dutton, 1961, pp 139–140.
32 *The Jerusalem Bible*, Ezekiel 1:26.
33 Kaplan, *Meditation and the Bible*, p 37.
34 Ibn 'Arabi, *The Meccan Revelations*, p 38.
35 Ibid p 131.
36 Cited in Kaplan, *Meditation and the Bible*, p 22, from Maimonides' classic book, *The Guide for the Perplexed*.

www.ingramcontent.com/pod-product-compliance
Lightning Source LLC
Chambersburg PA
CBHW030452010526
44118CB00011B/901